THE PITKIN REVIEW

SPRING 2018

Editor-in-Chief:	Ryan W. Shepard	
Associate Editors:	Snigdha Roy StarkadurSigurdarson	
Submissions Editor:	Edward Stephens	
Production Editor:	Aleesha Nash	
Copy Editors:	Heather Bartel Aaron Kiser Victoria Veldhoen	
Lead Editors:	Andrea Canaan Pamela Moore Dionne Kimi Hardesty Sean Hart Diana Smith Rush Ryan W. Shepard Victoria Veldhoen	Nonfiction Visual Art Drama Hybrid Fiction Critical Commentary Poetry
Web Chief:	Sean Hart	
Web Editor:	Nicole Goddard	
Social Media:	Victoria Veldhoen	
Distribution Manager:	Alana Jamison	
Genre Editors:	Critical Commentary	Jessica Cagle-Faber Kimi Hardesty Rae Quinn
	Drama	Diana Smith Rush Victoria Veldhoen Tina Ontiveros
	Fiction	Aurora Hurd Ryan Jakuboski Patrice Gerideau Abigail Crittenden Sam Rebelein
	Nonfiction	Smith Elder Hope Chandler Erik Rodgers

Poetry		Cate Gallivan
		Tina Ontiveros
		Alana Jamison
Visual Art		Erix Antoine
		Lindsay Clark
Hybrid		Emma Meistrich
		Jess Lewis
		Erik Rodger

Faculty Liaison: Beatrix Gates

Alumni Advisors: Jalyn Powell
Ariel Basom

Cover Art: "These Two There," Jennifer Skura

Contents

Letter From The Editor 1

In The Garden Pamela Moore Dionne 4

Comings And Goings Stacie Jenkins Townsend 6

The Third Thing That Damns Me Alana Jamison 7

Curves Smith Elder 12

How A Phoenix Feels Brett Townsend 13

Unreliable Narrators In O'connor's Everything That Rises Must Converge Victoria Veldhoen 17

I Didn't Know Kimi Hardesty 20

Moonstar Stacie Jenkins Townsend 22

Frozen Foods Ian August 23

The Death Room Diana Smith Rush 35

The Neighbor Tisha Gentry 39

Life Like Texture Jennifer Skura 40

Appetizer Pamela Moore Dionne 41

"Her Punishment Is Deerly Dire" Abigail Crittenden 43

Guten Tag Jessica Dickey 46

Headstanding Jaya Spier 56

Left-Hand Auto Anne Boaden 57

The Use Of An Unreliable Narrator In Vladimir Nabokov's Lolita Pamela Moore Dionne 61

Last Night Jaya Spier 64

His Body, My Regret Smith Elder 65

Redemption Stacie Jenkins Townsend 66

Adaptation: New Eyes Kimi Hardesty 68

Writing As A Means Of Accepting A Disability Diana Smith Rush 69

Day's End Tisha Gentry 74

Focus On Stacie Jenkins Townsend 75

Growing Kimi Hardesty 76

Shame Tisha Gentry 77

To His Others Smith Elder 78

I-5 Heaven Stacie Jenkins Townsend 80

Hybrid As An Expression Of Empathy Alana Jamison 81

Maldivian Fisherman Anne Boaden 93

LETTER FROM THE EDITOR

Hey, here's a challenge: Despite all the annotations, the papers, the creative writing, the mashed DELETE buttons, the multiple drafts, the day job, the night job, the home life, the commute, the political landscape, the societal problems you face, the struggles you've dealt with personally for years, the mountain that you personally climb -- submit work to the *Pitkin Review* in the hopes you'll get published. Hell, submit it to any periodical with those same hopes.

It ain't easy, my friend. I speak from experience. In the months leading up to even writing this note, I've been rejected five or six times for my own work. I feel it's good, but could be better. The "getting better" part is really the point; the fact that I can acknowledge that means that I've grown as a writer. And the fact that I'm working at it means that eventually, good things will come my way with time.

We initially had a theme for this issue, following the themed issue from Fall 2017. It was to be "Karma and Accountability," and given the political (if not emotional) state of the U.S. in 2017, we felt it was quite applicable. However, a lot of what we received -- and what ultimately made it into this issue -- didn't fall into that theme. Which is fine, of course, because the theme wasn't what we were weighing choices upon.

But the concept sticks with me. Karma. Accountability.

I admit, I'm more of a believer in karma when the guy who flies past me on the expressway, weaving between lanes, ends up pulled over by a state trooper. Driving past him with a big grin that I hope he sees -- to me, that's karma.

At the same time, I interpret karma as simply giving back,

working hard, exuding positivity. That's not magical, that's tangible. You work hard, you'll have something to show for your efforts -- usually what you were hoping for. You're considerate and kind to people, they'll reflect that back to you, and potentially others. You take other people's needs into consideration, they'll hopefully pass that generosity on to the next person in need.

Accountability. If you've got something to say, own it. If you stand behind the power of your convictions, don't waver. At the same time, take responsibility if what you're doing is wrong. Accountability builds and demonstrates character.

Mark Twain is attributed to the quote, "If you tell the truth, you don't have to remember anything." The same holds true for standing up for what you believe in. Filter through whatever fog is blocking what you truly believe in, and own it. It will be way easier to stand up for those beliefs. If you realize you've been doing something wrong, once you realize the proper path, get on it. Walk it, own it, believe in it, and you won't have to consciously make the decisions to back it -- you'll just *do it*. The accountability will come naturally.

So, as you're working toward becoming a better writer, as you're getting rejected (or accepted!), and the weight of every other possible stressor is looming down upon you, my only advice would be to keep working toward your goals. Walk that path, make right decisions, stick to your beliefs, be accountable.

The karmic celebration will be worth it at the end.

***

I want to take up a little more space to say thank you to all the students, alumni, and faculty who helped make the *Pitkin*

Review a fantastic issue. Not just by your writing contributions, but by your effort, your sense of teamwork, and your repeated offers to assist above and beyond what you were already doing. May you all have continued success in meeting *your* goals.

IN THE GARDEN
Pamela Moore Dionne

Say that perfection is
bound within a flawless ripe
tomato, a lovely woman,
the frequencies
of native bees.
Words like mosquitoes
nip along synapses,
each vowel falls against my ear
like monarch wings on petals,
their quick darts.
I hear sunlight
lick and salt my skin.
This is my first language.
        This,
filling me with heat and blood.
You cannot know this beauty.
It will not come again.

GURU
Anne Boaden

COMINGS AND GOINGS
Stacie Jenkins Townsend

THE THIRD THING THAT DAMNS ME
Alana Jamison

1. I didn't become a "rebel child" until I returned from my trip to another world, and it seemed like my parents grew afraid of my new otherworldly tendencies.

2. I grew up in Oklahoma, then moved to Kansas in high school. When we moved, my fear of a new place exhibited itself in my belief that attending a church that used instruments in worship would damn me.

   My fear exhibited itself in my insistence that my family visit a church that didn't use instruments in worship before they chose to attend a church that did.

   Then, I made friends in high school that took me to a church that filled me with the Holy Spirit, which was worse than attending a church that used instruments in worship.

   I don't mean to blaspheme. No, I just mean to say, that we all experience other worlds away from home, and change.

   I don't mean to blaspheme. No, I just mean that, if I was damned for attending a church that used instruments; I was damned again for attending a church that believed in the gifts of the Holy Spirit.

   No, I just meant to say that we all experience other worlds when we leave home, and when we leave home we experience change. Some people don't like change. Some people think change means you've taken the wrong path.

3. "Enter through the narrow gate; for the gate is wide and the way is broad that leads to destruction; and there are many who enter through it. For the gate is small and the

way is narrow that leads to life, and there are few who find it."

I used to think that this Bible verse (Matthew 7:13-14) referred to eternal life—to heaven and to hell—and I was convinced that very few people made it to heaven, which meant that my doubting thoughts and my questions about biblical interpretations and biblical translations and history, etc. might be the third thing that damns me.

Now, I don't know if that's what this verse means.

4. I don't know what I think about all of this. I don't know where to go from here.

5. One night ago, I told my husband that I've been thinking about what if I was in a homosexual relationship. I said that I've been wondering if I'd feel more fulfilled in a relationship with a woman.

Our relationship works because we don't hold back.

We were laying on the floor together. We were reconciling after an argument. He was stretching. The kids were asleep. We were going to bed.

"I wonder if I'd feel more fulfilled in a relationship with a woman."

6. I'm married, so I can handle it. I'm not afraid, so I can handle it.

7. I was a virgin on my wedding night in the sense that I'd been the only one who touched me.

You know what I mean.

"That's normal," she said to me, when I finally confessed to my high school mentor that I struggled with masturbation during middle school and high school. "That's normal," my dad said, when I finally confessed the same to him and my mother.

I'm having sex with myself, I'd think.

I had an issue with sex as a kid. I didn't have a good understanding about how my body worked, and as far as I was concerned my entire body was sending me to hell.

"Maybe you didn't get the affection you needed from your mother as a child, that's why you sought attachment from other girls your age."

I wasn't gay, but my high school best friend's mother constantly lectured my friend and me on why we should be careful when were around each other.

We were affectionate. We shared a bed when I slept over. We weren't gay. We weren't having sex. My friend was obsessed with boys. She loved the movie "The Notebook."

I wasn't gay, but after high school and some college my parents didn't want me moving to Kansas City to live with my new best friend and her family.

I needed to finish school.

They didn't want me following her to college.

"That sounds too much like marriage to me," my father said.

I did move to Kansas City after an emotional upheaval with my parents, and my friend and I shared a bed for six months. We shared intimate moments. We did life together. We never had sex. Neither of us were gay. I had a boyfriend to prove it.

But the neighbors across the street saw us hugging.

The neighbors across the street mocked my friend. They said "She's gay."

8. Two nights ago, I fell in a heap on the floor after arguing with my husband. I fought back the temptation to say "I hate you" again to him, and said "I hate this" instead. I hammered the door frame with my fists and wailed like a child. He carried me screaming to the bedroom while holding our infant son. While I lay on the bed saying "I'm sorry. I'm sorry." over and over again, he patted me on the back to console me the way we comfort our children when they are distressed.

Maybe I can't handle it. Whatever "it" is.

But I did heal while lying in a heap on the bed; like an open wound knit shut I connected so absolutely with my feelings and became a child—honest and vulnerable—I stopped hiding and stopped blaming. I began repeating "I don't know. I don't know." and accepting that as a good answer.

9. Once, I told my husband, "Maybe I do have homosexual tendencies."

When I see certain woman, I experience an intense longing that I've never felt when looking at a man. Does this mean, I'm sexually attracted to women?

Last night I told my husband, "I wonder if I'd feel more fulfilled in a relationship with women."

"I'd be sad if you left," he said.

I could never leave him.

"I've come to realize that no one can fulfill me the way I need them to," he said.

That's comforting to hear.

10. Are men and women both Christ's bride?

    I can't answer that question, now, but I do feel something deeply.

    Does hell even exist?

    "For the Kingdom of God is already among you."

11. It's morning and the sun is shining through the trees, and I'm wondering where I should go from here. I am reading inside and a green grasshopper attracted by my lamp light jumps onto my shoulder then off it.

12. I imagine my hand open, palm facing up to the sky, fingers outstretched away from my body. Light comes up out of my hand, as though I am a supernatural being.

    What if we are all more than we seem?

13. Today, I discovered that my right hand is bruised because of hammering the door frame with my fist and wailing like a child.

14. Last night, my husband came home and I pulled him close to me. We kissed. We touched. We spent the entire night blissfully close. Our sex echoed the deep desires in both of us—"I want to know. I want to know."—and we felt full and intense and alive.

CURVES
Smith Elder

On the moon
I weigh 28 pounds.

On earth
I can only be beautiful
if I lose twice that.

But who's to say
that the moon hasn't got it right?
On the moon we can leap walls
and the ground is soft,
bearing us up like
a child's trampoline—
white cratered innocence.

On the moon
I fall just like a feather—
      slow
      And
      Straight
      down.

HOW A PHOENIX FEELS
Brett Townsend

Before retirement funds and detailed monthly budgets, before life insurance and car payments, back when we were living on dreams and good circumstance you would say, "I want to be free," and I would say, "You already are." And I would hold you close as we fell asleep. In the morning we might have a plan. In the morning we might say, "This place looks nice," or, "I've always wanted to go there."

We would book the tickets, or fill the tank, or rent the U-Haul, and stuff it full. We would stay for a week or a year or a day wherever we went, no thought of return. And yet, we always did return, it was always in our cards, back to life as it was, or as it would eventually be. And now, what have we become? Are we now free? What have we built that isn't already crumbling? Where do we go from here? To the Costco? A big adventure? Ten trips around the house? Cutting the lawn.

You stand at the sink and complain that I haven't washed yet this week. I take the pile of clean clothes from the bed and move it to the floor. Too tired to fold. On my side of the bed, I steal the covers without knowing, you complain. I get up early to cook for our family. I bring you coffee in bed.

I beg for the love we used to share, the kind that didn't feel like work. You say your stomach isn't feeling right; you talk about your mother's husband. I turn away. I set the alarm, and turn off the light. Your voice feels hollow in the dark; you promise tomorrow night will be different. It isn't; we both succumb to the lullaby of a movie neither of us are interested in. Why do we watch?

I'm trying to lose some weight. I think, maybe if I lose some weight she'll want me again. I'm probably right. She lies and says she still wants me. Nice of her. Still, it would feel good to be wanted.

In the morning, like sardines, we and our two boys are stacked in bed. I never hear them come in. My back hurts and your neck is out. Is there a cheap chiropractor in this town? Why doesn't our insurance cover stuff like that?

You're frustrated that one of the boys wet their bed, second time this week. I don't know what to say. Tonight, he'll wet *our* bed, too. The way you talk about it makes me feel like it's my fault. Is it?

You get the boys to school on time. There are days when that doesn't happen, and their teacher is threatening suspension. Good grief; for the money we're paying a few minutes shouldn't fucking matter. Maybe it does, but still.

Now your car is having issues; the check engine light is on, and the transmission sounds funny. I take it for a service, hoping that will do the trick. Half a paycheck, and it still won't shift. Half a life ago, and it wouldn't have mattered. I'll have to take back the old Dodge my nephew is borrowing. You can use my car. We can't afford it, all this... modernity.

I've got a meeting tonight. Yes, there will be beer, but I promise not to drink too much. *Too* much, what is *too* much? I don't know. I have four and tell you I had three. You say you think I had five. I pass out and you read a book about Waldorf education. It's exhausting, being alive.

I've been wondering where I went. Where a me I could recognize flew off to. I feel I've lost little bits of myself along the tracks, and now I know there's something left, but I don't know what it is. Maybe this is how a phoenix feels, just before he is finally reduced to ash. Or maybe this is how a bonfire feels, when all that's left is coals. Maybe this is what it feels like to drown.

I used to eat a whole pizza by myself. I used to stay up all night at least once a month. I would often drink seven or nine or twelve, and the next day I was always fine. The next day I would run seven or nine or twelve. I would stay up late again; I would love someone with abandon, unprotected and unafraid. I loved many. Many loved me. You loved me too.

You say I should get it snipped. I agree, but am afraid. You say I could never bear a child; I agree, but am afraid. You say it's no big deal; guys do it all the time; you push and cajole. I'm scared; am I not allowed?

Is this what it means to age? Is it forever and always being stuck in the best and worst of the past? Is it seeing a future in checkout lines and parking lots, feeble bones, struggling to carry a sack of food. Am I passing my future self on the road and wondering, "Why's he still driving?" I peek over the horizon of years to where I'm headed, a toothless and flaccid place, a place that seemed in earlier times as as if it weren't real. I am horrified. I am afraid.

My heart is a melancholy dream, and my mind is all troubled waters. My body, though still capable enough, is shifting. Don't eat *too* much of this, none at all of that, no coffee after four. Smoking will kill you. I drink three, and the next day is a headache. I drink five, and I feel like a zombie. Beyond that I might as well stay in bed. Even when I don't drink, even then, I'm hurting all the time. I'm wondering about all the hurting; I can't stop wondering. Is it a pulled muscle or kidney stones? Is thirty-three too young for a stroke? Did I really live *that* hard and fast?

I think I'm folding in on myself. I used to want nothing more than to be out among the people, new people, speaking new words, holding new hands, tasting new lips. I used to want to find new places, to be lost in them, to find myself in them. Lately I stay at home; I stay in my room; I don't want anything new, but somehow the old has lost its flavor, too. Somehow, I've become accustomed to the bland, to the ordinary, to the tasteless, and I am bland too.

I look at my teeth after brushing, and I see years of neglect. I see stains and chips and spaces where there should be none. I think we should have three sets of teeth. It would be nice, to lose them all around forty, and grow some new after learning their value. That's one change I would make, if I were God.

I tried talking to you about sex, I was trying be honest about my needs. "You're a big boy," you said, "you can take care of yourself." You started lecturing me; you sounded like my mom. Dear God, what the fuck have we become? You were in the shower, and I was on the commode; you said we were boring now. You asked for a courtesy flush, and I obliged. I didn't say anything. I wanted to say something, but what I wanted to say would have lost me the *privilege* of sharing a house with you and the kids. I climbed in the shower, and you got out.

I'm shaving, and the mirror keeps fogging up. I wipe away just enough to see the patch of neck I'm working. When I finish I try to find myself there in reflection. I see an outline where I should be. I see the tile on the wall behind. I see you float in and out for deodorant and medication, but I'm not there, and I wonder where it is I've gone.

UNRELIABLE NARRATORS IN O'CONNOR'S EVERYTHING THAT RISES MUST CONVERGE
Victoria Veldhoen

If a character tells a story that cannot be taken at face value, he or she is considered to be an unreliable narrator. They may be unreliable when detailing the events of a story, or simply in their interpretation of them. Although any story which isn't told from a third-person omniscient point of view can be considered at least somewhat untrustworthy, some narrators are more questionable than others. O'Connor's *Everything That Rises Must Converge* is a collection of short stories that contains a multitude of deluded protagonists, whose own biases are so evident throughout the text that I often wanted to hit them in the head. Often unlikeable, the characters in O'Connor's stories tend to seethe with self-importance and a hatred of their own family members. Although the protagonists' criticisms of others are not always without merit, their inability to see their own (often very similar) flaws make for intriguing case studies on how to successfully write unreliable narrators well.

The most important way to demonstrate a narrator's lack of credibility is to have them state something as fact which the reader can then immediately discern as falsehood. O'Connor does this beautifully in her first story "Everything That Rises Must Converge," where she details the relationship between Julian and his mother, Mrs. Chestny. The basic plot of the story is that after the racial integration of public transport in the South, Mrs. Chestny insists that Julian accompany her weekly visit to the Y. Through remarks said out loud and his own internal monologue, we soon come to understand that Julian thinks of himself as worldly and his mother as an old-fashioned racist. There is *some* truth to what he says, as Mrs.

Chestny is undoubtedly racist. Her uneasiness at racial integration is obvious when she boards the bus, sees only white people, and remarks with relief, "I see we have the bus to ourselves" (10). And yet, Julian is not much better. He dreams of bringing home a "beautiful suspiciously Negroid woman" only to see his mother's reaction (15). He doesn't see Black Americans as people, but only as one-dimensional characters which he can use to demonstrate his own superiority over his mother.

Julian is obsessed with being better than his mother. So much so, that it permeates almost every thought he has throughout their short bus ride together. He believes that she lives "according to the laws of her own fantasy world" and yet, Julian does the exact same thing (11). However, he cannot see this about himself, as detailed summarily in the following passage:

Most miraculous of all, instead of being blinded by love for her as she was for him, he had cut himself emotionally free from her and could see her with complete objectivity. He was not dominated by his mother. (12)

These lines are hilarious because they show just how self-absorbed and delusional Julian really is. He has done nothing but compare himself to his mother the entire trip, and yet he somehow believes that he's not dominated by her. Julian's character is the very definition of an unreliable narrator, and O'Connor spells it out by showing us exactly how his own thoughts disagree with who he undoubtedly is as a character.

 Another way to demonstrate unreliability is simply to show the narrator having thoughts that most reasonable people can discern as unrealistic. O'Connor does this well in the story "The Lame Shall Enter First," which is a tale about a widower named Sheppard who is unable to understand his son Norton's grief for his mother a year after her death. When Norton breaks into tears after Sheppard callously references that at least "your mother is not in the state penitentiary," Sheppard thinks to himself that his wife "had been dead for over a year and a child's grief should not last so long" (146). A year is not enough time to get over the death of someone as important as a mother, especially to a young child. If anything, Norton is the one acting normal here, and Sheppard is the one acting oddly. And yet, he continues to categorize unfairly his son as selfish, constantly comparing him to Rufus, a young juvenile delinquent. Even though Rufus is consistently abhorrent to Sheppard, saying that he "don't know his left hand from his right," Sheppard continues to think of Rufus as the one with real potential and his own son as the lost cause (155). He doesn't realize his mistake until it's much too late, and he's confronted with his son hanging from the attic.

Part of why unreliable narrators work so well is because all of us can see ourselves within them, no matter how abhorrent. Every individual holds within themselves views that are false, and it's usually only through our own personal tragedies (though not generally as tragic as O'Connor's characters) that we grow to mature and realize this. Thus, in writing them, we write ourselves.

O'Connor, Flannery. *Everything That Rises Must Converge.* New York: Farrar, Straus, and Giroux, 1993, c1965., 1993. Print.

I DIDN'T KNOW
Kimi Hardesty

My father came from nothing, his mother abandoned him at the age of 16 when his own daddy died. Despite his upbringing, he made himself something. He said some people are lazy and don't want to work, like the Negroes and Mexicans. I was born in the mid-fifties, to Republican parents. I didn't know.

We had a second place, a farm, an hour from the city and there was a banner across the road, as you exited the highway, to go under the overpass, on the way to our weekend home.

The banner read:

The blackest land and the whitest people. I didn't know.

Third grade. We moved to the country. They were bused from their homes, their communities, so it would all seem even. The first blacks came into school and I saw them as something foreign and worried what might happen if I touched their skin. Black water moccasins like those in the ponds behind our house on the two-lane road. Dangerous. Dirty. Don't touch. The black rubbing off on my fingers or maybe not. My only exposure was my daddy's words. I didn't know.

One-day tall Daisy Mae sat at her desk in one of my old dresses. I didn't mind but it didn't feel right, like she had on the wrong skin, the blue flowers running down her black shiny arms that glistened. I wondered how she got my dress, and my mother didn't tell me she'd donated my old clothes. I didn't know.

Later there was talk of Daisy Mae bleeding and red rags, and I had my Kotex kit ready and waiting for me to become a woman. I couldn't wait and she didn't have a chance, and soon

Daisy Mae's belly grew and grew and then she was gone. All we shared was the sky. I didn't know.

Education. Anticipation. Privilege. Clean white soaking up red. | All bloody.

My father planted an acre of cotton on our land. He wanted me and my sister to learn about cattle and crops, and of course we were going to college. When the bolls popped open, displaying the white fluffy cotton, they came. They were in dirty clothes and wore rags around their heads and carried sacks and their backs were bent all day, under a sun that blazed.

Injustice. Heat. Disparity

Arms moving back and forth, back and forth. My sister and did some picking, but the rough bolls hurt our hands and we stopped, but the pickers kept going despite the sun and the tender fingers. I didn't know.

Come high school graduation, there was Ollie and Josephine in the class picture. Two black bodies among the small sea of white and some, like me, didn't see any difference in them although my daddy kept up with his talking. I didn't know.

After college, I worked for my daddy's business. One day a black man walked in the door. He stated he was there to take me to lunch, and my daddy got up from his desk and told the man

NO

And the man said he understood and walked out the door. Four years of exposure and college and away from home. Small town don't know any better and all those like-minded people and the 50's and 60's became the 70's.

And then I did know. It took a long time.

MOONSTAR
Stacie Jenkins Townsend

FROZEN FOODS
Ian August

A Short Play

Cast of Characters:
CAROL – 40s, Mother and Housewife
LINDA – 40s, Mother and Housewife

Place: Aisle 11 of the Superfood Market
Time: Now-ish

(Lights up on the frozen foods aisle of the local Superfood Market, clear glass case doors line the path, each one containing brightly colored packages obscured by thin layers of frost. CAROL, 40s, a mother and housewife, stands among them, a plastic basket at her feet. She holds a frozen TV dinner in her hands. She stares at it, blankly.)

(She stares. She stares.)

CAROL:

Four for the price of one.

(LINDA, 40s, also a mother and housewife and part time real estate agent, enters. She sees CAROL.)

LINDA:

Carol? Is that you?

(CAROL does not respond.)

Oh my God, Carol? Carol! I haven't seen you since the PTA meeting three weeks ago! How have you been? How's Jessie? Has she had her ballet recital yet? I ended up returning the toe shoes and tutu when Virginia told me she would rather dig up moss in the cracks of the sidewalk than go back to ballet. I took her in the back yard and gave her a stick and watched her go to town. She was on the front stoop for nearly three hours. I practically read a whole novel! Well, it was a novella, but who's counting?

(CAROL does not respond.)

She is exhausting though—running around like she's being chased by a rabid ocelot. Zip! Zip! Zip! I literally fell asleep at Tiffany's birthday party at Funderland last week. Literally. Asleep. Standing. Next to the skee ball. Virginia and Molly from church found me passed out upright like a horse clutching a wad of tickets in my teeth and the straw from my Diet Sprite poking out of a hole in my sweater. Can you believe it? I looked insane!

(CAROL does not respond.)

Really insane! Hahaha!

(LINDA finally notices CAROL's catatonic gaze.)

Carol? Carol, honey, are you okay?

(CAROL does not respond)

Carol?

(LINDA reaches for the frozen dinner, and the moment she touches it, CAROL jolts upright. She looks up to LINDA.)

CAROL:

Linda?

LINDA:

Carol? What... what happened?

CAROL:

I... I don't know. I just... I just...

LINDA:

Carol, are you okay? Do you want me to call the manager?

CAROL:

No, I'm fine. Really, I am.

LINDA:

You gave me quite a shock.

CAROL:

I know. I'm sorry.

LINDA:

What was—what were you doing?

CAROL:

Oh, Lin—Oh...

I'm not sure. I remember I was standing here, looking for the Hungrifriend Dinners.

LINDA:

I love those dinners.

CAROL:

Me, too.

LINDA:

The Salisbury steak with the peas and carrots? Yum!

CAROL:

I know.

LINDA:

And look! They're on sale! (CAROL blanches.) Four for the price of one!

CAROL:

(a realization) That's it! That's what it was!

LINDA:

What what was?

CAROL:

I was reaching in to grab a few Hungrifriend Dinners—the fried chicken ones that Bill likes best. The ones that have the little pocket of corn and the little pocket of potatoes and the tiny cocoa scented mock-brownie patty...

LINDA:

Frank loves those, too.

CAROL:

And then I remembered: I paid full price for those last week.

LINDA:

I... I don't follow.

CAROL:

Last week—last week I bought four of these Hungrifriend Dinners—and they cost four dollars a box. I spent sixteen dollars on these last week. Sixteen! And today—I look over and see that they're four for four dollars? It's ridiculous!

LINDA:

I know! What a deal!

CAROL:

And then I thought, there must be something wrong with these. A lapsed expiration date, a reduced number of chicken bits, the potatoes are made of wallpaper paste. Why else would they be so much less expensive this week than last?

LINDA:

It's just a sale, Carol. There are always sales on these things.

CAROL:

But why? Why should they cost me a dollar a box this week when last week I spent four times as much? Who makes up those rules? Who gets to decide that the Hungrifriend Dinners I buy this week should be worth so much less than the ones from last week? And why are they so cheap? If there's nothing wrong with them—if they're the same boxed chicken dinners from last week—well then—what the hell is going on? It makes no sense! And then it came to me:

(CAROL takes a pause. She looks up)

There is no such thing as God.

LINDA:

What?

CAROL:

Don't you see, Linda? If there was a God, if there was an almighty figure presiding over everything—every birth, every death—if there was a grand organizer up in heaven planning and plotting and dictating the motions of our existence—then how could that explain the randomness of it all? Four for the price of one? Four for the price of one?

LINDA:

For God's sake, Carol—it's just a sale!

CAROL:

But it isn't, is it? It's not just a sale. Because it's also children getting cancer and wars in the Middle East and famine and drought and flooding and tornadoes! It's the Thomases getting divorced and the giant goiter on Jenny Mueller's neck and that boy who lives down the street who has three eyes and seven nipples. It's random, don't you see, Linda? It's completely arbitrary! There's no plan, because there's no planner! God does not exist!

LINDA:

I bet Pastor Jim wouldn't be too pleased to hear you say that.

CAROL:

Fuck Pastor Jim, Linda! Fuck him right in the eye! And do you know why? Because if God doesn't exist, if God isn't real—and I'm pretty sure this (she grabs the frozen dinner from LINDA's hand and shakes it in the air) proves that God isn't real—then what is real? What is reality?

LINDA:

Carol—you—you're talking nonsense!

CAROL:

Am I, Lin? Or are you even here? Are you real, Linda?

LINDA:

Of course, I'm real! I'm buying stool softeners! Why would I do that if I weren't real?

CAROL:

Maybe, Linda, maybe you don't exist. Maybe none of this exists. This basket, this dinner, this entire aisle is a series of electrical currents in my brain attempting to convince me that it's all real. But none of it—not even you—exist. You are simply a series of random signals to my brain. You only exist if I can perceive you. The minute I turn—

(She does so—the lights shift. Only the objects in front of her remain in light. Everything else is bathed in darkness.)

The objects behind me cease to be. And when I turn the other way...

(She does so—the lights shift. Only the objects in front of her remain in light. Everything else is bathed in darkness.)

The world appears to me born anew, and the things I no longer observe are gone forever.

LINDA:

But they're not, Carol—they're all still there!

CAROL:

Says the voice inside my brain that I have recently named "Linda."

LINDA:

That was my grandmother's name!

CAROL:

Your grandmother doesn't exist. The world in which I live is confined to my ability to perceive it. If I do not see it, it cannot be. I am at the center of the universe!

(CAROL turns out to the audience. The stage becomes the darkness of space—and millions of stars appear around them. LINDA stares out in wonder. When they speak, their voices echo.)

If I do not hear you, you have not spoken. If I do not see you, you are not there. Even touch is not a touch—it is merely a false sensory experience activated by convincing my brain that my nerve endings have been stimulated.

LINDA:

This is like that Keanu Reeves movie.

CAROL:

The one with the bus?

LINDA:

The one with the robots.

CAROL:

The Notebook had robots?

LINDA:

I think that was Ryan Gosling.

CAROL:

It doesn't matter. None of them exist.

LINDA:

But Carol—if nothing exists but you—then how do you know if you exist?

(CAROL stops, stunned—behind her, a super nova suddenly bursts into being, a brilliant explosion of light envelops the stage. And then darkness.)

CAROL:

Oh my God—you're right. I don't exist.

There is nothing anywhere. There is nothing anywhere.

(CAROL and LINDA begin to float in the darkness)

LINDA:

Carol!

CAROL:

I thought I heard a voice. But I don't exist. Maybe the voice is the only part of me that's real.

LINDA:

Carol!

CAROL:

Do I respond to it? Can I respond? Or is it just a gust of galactic wind, screaming my name into the nothingness of the universe?

LINDA:

Carol! Goddammit! Listen to me!

CAROL:

How foolish I was to think I could contain the universe within me. I know only too late that I am the neither the universe nor its vessel. I am merely an echo of its emptiness.

(LINDA slaps CAROL across the face with the Hungrifriend Dinner. The lights return to normal. LINDA and CAROL stand in the frozen food aisle of the Superfood Market. Beat.)

CAROL:

That hurt.

LINDA:

Then you exist, don't you?

CAROL:

I, uh...

LINDA:

You want me to slap your face again?

CAROL:

No.

LINDA:

Do you want me to step on your foot? Or punch your breast?

CAROL:

Not really.

LINDA:

Why not?

CAROL:

It hurts.

LINDA:

Carol. If it hurts, it's real.

(Beat)

Maybe you should go home and lie down for a while.

CAROL:

Yes. You know? I think... I think you may be right. I think that might make me feel a bit better.

LINDA:

Of course, it will, hon.

(LINDA picks up CAROL's basket and hands it to her.)

Be safe getting home. And give Bill and Jessie my love, okay?

CAROL:

Okay.

LINDA:

See you next week at the PTA meeting?

(CAROL doesn't answer. She exits, still a little dazed. LINDA watches her go, and then looks down at her hands. She holds the box of Hungrifriend Dinner. She looks at it, and reaches for the freezer case.)

Four for the price of one.

(She giggles. And then stops. She brings her hand back. She stares at the box in her hands.)

Four for the price of one.

(She stares. She stares.)

(Blackout.)

END OF PLAY

THE DEATH ROOM
Diana Smith Rush

Last week I was asked to organize my friend Erica's house to help prepare for her death. Since her Stage Four Breast Cancer diagnosis two years ago, I have been honored to be asked to help her and her family with a variety of tasks. I have brought meals, cleaned her bathrooms and driven her kids to events. Each time I helped I felt the joy of knowing I was making her life easier. I was not thinking of the end but instead my focus was on that moment in time. Then she updated her blog with the hashtag, *#monthsnotyears.*

I am new to hashtags, and I still don't know what to do with them. I tried to scoot my laptop's mouse over one once and click on it, but wasn't sure what I was supposed to do with the links appearing on my screen. Since hashtags have to be written as one word, they sometimes need multiple readings to decode. Not this one.

Her blog post talked about the latest test results confirming what she already believed. There were cancer lesions on her brain. This news combined with the terminal cancer she already had, meant her time was running out. The prognosis changing from years to months, meant it was happening fast.

Erica was like nobody I had ever met before. When our paths crossed at a homeschool program years ago, I felt myself being pulled towards her as if she was magnetized. So did everyone else. Wherever she was, Erica held court. Crowds of kids and parents gathered around as her energy filled the space. She was full of life. *Is* full of life.

When she got her diagnosis she actually said she felt "chosen." The news came to me in a message on Facebook.

Stage Four. Terminal. Inoperable. *Chosen.* I chose to believe if anyone could beat it, it would be Erica. I didn't research her type of cancer or check out the statistics. I didn't need to because I was sure she was the exception. But here I was, preparing her home so she could die in it.

"So, this is my death room," she said as I walked into her house, ready to clean. I followed her to what used to serve as her office, but now was earmarked for something else. The space was mostly empty, save a wall of shelves on one side. She gestured to the shelves that were heavy with books and computer equipment. "These shelves were put put up. Before. They will get cleaned off."

I had been part of the committee formed to clean and organize when she first found out she was sick. The office was my jurisdiction. I waded through piles of drawings her children had made through the years, unopened bills and stacks of medical paperwork. I threw things out when she wasn't looking, trying to lighten her load. Trying to make her a space to live in.

On the wall across from the shelves, masking tape outlined two large rectangles. "What are those?" I asked, genuinely curious.

"" We are having windows put in. I wanted a screen porch but there isn't time."

I felt myself get warm and my heart started beating hard in my chest. Her words were hurting me, but I knew I couldn't admit that out loud.

"That will be really pretty," I said instead.

She led me to the basement and explained what she needed

done. She directed me to overflowing boxes, broken down on the corners from mice and mildew. "Can you look through these and find any art the kids made?" Of course, I could. Anything.

We worked side by side in the basement. While she dug through the boxes, I snuck glances at her. Most of the time, there was a small grin on her face. Sometimes I caught her clutching a photograph to her chest and closing her eyes. I wondered how she really felt knowing her time on earth was now down to months.

Halfway through our time she announced she needed a rest. I was left in the basement knee deep in her memories. The memories she didn't want to leave for her husband and children to have to go through.

I have my own memories of Erica. She is the godmother to my first grandchild, the baby she cradles and declares makes her feel the closest she can ever feel to God. The moment she met my disabled son and told me he was perfect, and we should all be more like him. When she held me and told me that *I* inspire *her*.

I completed my shift and walked up to the death room on my way out. I wanted to stand in the doorway and take it in. I wanted to absorb it so I could remember each detail and hold onto it later when the news came that she was in it, dying. Instead I walked outside with Erica where she showed me the ATV her family bought her in order to check another box off her bucket list.

Her husband and son took me on a ride through the woods while I gripped the bar over my head and closed my eyes like Erica had in the basement, holding onto her memories.

The death room will wait and when it is time, the windows will be in and the shelves will be clear. The boxes in the basement will be reorganized by categories like photographs and children's art. And I will close my eyes and have a small grin on my face and think of my friend.

THE NEIGHBOR
Tisha Gentry

His heart fell on the drive way
She overheard her parents say
he'd been dying for a while now
Scared
At age 7
She wondered if she'd been dying
for a while now too

LIFE LIKE TEXTURE
Jennifer Skura

APPETIZER
Pamela Moore Dionne

at the Folk Life Festival
we met a barefoot man
popping young slugs
into his mouth
describing the taste

      broccoli   grass

sage   basil

    cabbage

They taste like what they eat,
he tells us and offers one
as it traverses the palm of his hand
an innocent cresting man's
thenar eminence below his thumb

    My mind runs a video I once saw.
    Two leopard slugs mate in midair,
    dangle from a strand of conjoined
    mucus, a transparent, shimmering rope.
    They spread tiny flightless wing flaps,
    spiral round and round each other.
    Both are male and female capable.
    Each extends an organ,
    entwine in milky translucence,
    form a bell flower and trade sperm.
    It is an incredibly long sex scene
    just the right amount of slow and easy.
    The small creature I am offered
    glistens in shimmering slime,

>   refracting liquid light regardless
>   of possible destinies.
>   I am once again aware of awe.

And so, I decline the man's offer
to sip at the cup of paradise.
Not even should it taste
of caviar.

"HER PUNISHMENT IS DEERLY DIRE"
Abigail Crittenden

      They, Artemis and her nymphs,
Sat upon the seats of the booth
at the Lakeside Tavern Pub
They sat all together arrayed
Around their Lady as in times of old
Lathing their minds and souls
Of the day's wearies and worries
      When the door should open
And men counting six strode in,
Actaeon and his pack,
Built tall and thick and strode
As if they truly owned whatever place
Which was forced to house them
Actaeon, being a Hunter of
The Most Dangerous Prey, scented the air
For the sex he deemed fairer than his
And finding a booth of beauties manned
By a woman as feminine as she was butch
He decided to take his chance for the night
      He ignored the scent of blood
Which hung over Lady Artemis and her band
And interrupted their beloved drinks
And bellowed, "Maiden Fair, why dost thou not
Sit upon my visage? I am sure it is a fairer seat then
The one upon which you sit," with a smile as large
As he believed his charisma to be
      The nymphs were uncomfortable
And unamused, having dealt with his like for
Bygone numbers of centuries but never getting
Used to the level of smarm they brought
      Artemis looked at him, angered by

The utter gall he had to interrupt them and to disrupt
Her beloved people, and said in her great voice,
"You speak as one without any mind of what
A woman must face, so why do I not show you,
Fair sir, just what you are missing?" and with a snap
Of her beautiful white fingers, Actaeon was no more
        For in the place where once stood a
Man built like a house for fecal matter
Now stood a woman as fair as she was
Built with a body those who desired her
Would have sexual thoughts about
        His pack took one look
Upon what had been their master
But was now their favorite prey,
With minds as fogged of thought
As the night of a kegger,
And like meat thrown to the dogs,
Up went their howling barks,
Their laughter as horrid as their manners,
And soon, Actaeon was pulled back from the booth
Then, he was pulled back from the bar,
With true fear in his eyes as he realized
That what he had done to others
Would be happening to him,
And as the doors closed
The night was rent asunder by a
        Single
        Sharp
        Scream
And Artemis's punishment,
For a night interrupted with her ladies,
Had been fulfilled
Perhaps too harshly to some

But so was the will of a Goddess
And to be unquestioned
Was her Law

GUTEN TAG
Jessica Dickey

(An ASMR artist is filming a session. She's in a recording studio. That she built in her own home. Because she makes ASMR videos so often and they get so many views that she earns her living for it. She's a pro. Her make up is frighteningly precise. Her face looks like Barbie made a baby with an Elf and then dipped it in Teflon. Which is to say she has a strange beauty.

She speaks into the microphone and makes maternal eye contact with an unseen camera. She moves her arms and hands in slow, soothing gestures, like she's caressing an unseen face.)

CORINNE
Good evening.
Thank you so much for joining me tonight.
I hope you are wearing your headphones
So I can be as close to you as possible…
Good.

Tonight I'm going to relax you
I'm going to use some very relaxing techniques
Relaxing sounds
Relaxing words
That I hope you will enjoy.

First I'm going to start with some very relaxing hand movements
That I hope will make you feel

(She leans closer to the mic, whispers)

Relaxed.

*(She pulls back and smiles.
Then she moves closer to the mic and whispers again)*

I sense that something could be troubling you.
You are carrying
a weight, yes?
I'd like to provide you with some comfort today.
If you'll allow me.

(She leans closer to the mic)

I hope you trust me.

(And closer still)

You're safe with me.

(Back to original distance, she flashes a smile)

Let me tell you about what I have in store for you today.

(She picks up a wooden hairbrush. All of her movements are slow and sensual.)

Many of you have written me
about how much you love this hairbrush.
And I thank you for your messages.
I love hearing from you.
This is a wonderful hairbrush.
Made of wood.
Very natural.

(extra whispered)

I love wood.

(She taps the wood with her fingernails.)

So, we'll be working with that today.

But first I'd like to start with —

(She produces a drink with ice in it.)

Some carbonated water with ice.

Can you hear that?

(She puts the drink to the mic—you can hear bubbles fizzing and ice tinkling. She smiles gently, sensually.)

Isn't that wonderful?

(After a moment of fizzing and tinkling)

In this world,
where there is so much struggle,
so much noise and loss
I hope our time together brings you peace.
You deserve peace.

(She puts down the drink)

Now I'm going to give you a little head massage.
To relax you.

(She leans in to the mic, whispers)

Let go of that weight.

(She rubs her fingers on the microphone.)

When I was a little girl,
we used to lay in the farthest edge of the field of my elementary school,
where the grass was thickest.

This was during recess.
We would lay in the grass and take turns
dragging blades of grass up and down our arms,
very gently,
clouds overhead.
I liked My Little Pony
and the cartoon Jem
And the Holograms.
I liked warm milk with cacao and honey.
I liked my grandmother's fleshy arms
and our cat Guten Tag.
I liked my little room in the attic
On Rauscha Street.

(sadly)

Nothing lasts in this world.

Now we're going to brush my hair.
Would you like that?
Let's begin—

(JOSH suddenly enters the studio.)

JOSH
Oh shit. Sorry—is this…?

CORINNE
--- Hello…?

JOSH
Wow. It's really you.

CORINNE
--- Who are you?

JOSH

Oh god-- Are you recording??

CORINNE (looking around)
I-- ???--- How did you get in here?

JOSH
I'm sorry-- the door was just-- open--?

(She doesn't appear panicked, but her feelings probably play out on a much smaller stage than the rest of us.)

CORINNE
Do—do I know you?—

JOSH
Uhhh

CORINNE *(still quiet)*
You should probably go.

JOSH
Yeah, sure, I get that.
This was weird.
I mean, *I'm* weird, but this was *extra*--...

(realizing what a bad idea this was)

Clearly, I didn't think this through.
I just wanted to-- Sorry if I-- disturbed you, or...

(He starts to leave, then stops)

Can I just say one thing before I leave?
I watch your videos every night.

(She holds up a hand to interrupt him. Then--)

CORINNE

Can you--?

(She gestures for him to use the microphone)

Please.

JOSH
Oh. Okay.

(He speaks into the microphone)

I watch your videos every night.
Ever since my mom died...
I can't go to sleep.
But I found your videos and I'm better.
I'm getting better.
When I saw you at the Wegman's, I just knew it was you.
Except—you didn't have the two lights?
In your eyes. The two lights?
Do you know what I'm--?
In the videos, your videos, you have these-- two lights-- in your eyes.
Like literally in each eye there are two lights.
Probably from these lights in the booth?
And one is a larger circular white light, with a black center,
And the other is a fuzzier smaller light, down and to the left of the bigger light.
Your eyes in the videos...
So pale they're almost colorless?
With huge black pupils in the middle
And these perfect spikey eyelashes
Your make-up is *really* precise.
And inside your eyes
in the black black of your pupils
are these two lights.

Like spaceships.
Little serene spaceships.

(Beat. She recognizes him!)

CORINNE
You're the check out guy.
Aren't you?
At the Wegmans?

JOSH
You recognize me?

CORINNE
You—you helped me find the capers.
They weren't with the condiments.

JOSH
No, we keep 'em in the baking aisle?
Yeah, it's like—a really bad choice.

CORINNE
It is.

JOSH
I can't believe you recognize me.
That was like a month ago.

CORINNE
I recognize your beard.

JOSH
My beard?

CORINNE
The front right section of your beard is sort of—um—
Unruly?

It grows faster than the rest-- so it—um-- sticks out.
Like a snaggle tooth.
But a beard.
Beard hairs.

JOSH
It does? I didn't know that.
Gross.
I'm Josh.

CORINNE
I don't like to be touched.

JOSH
Okay.

CORINNE
Can you...?
Can you put your beard on the microphone?
Put your beard on the—yes--
And then rub it
side to side,
Side to side

(He does this. Slowly. He's not sure what he's doing, but she likes it.)

That's right. Yes.
And then—can you—
Can you rub the snaggle tooth beard hairs—yes—right yes--
Side to side, side to--
Yes.

*(He does this for a moment. Then he stops.
A pregnant pause between them.)*

JOSH
I remember thinking,
She needs a hug.
You wore slippers and a hoodie, frowning at the capers,
From the end of the aisle I watched.
You were so
hugless.

CORINNE
Will you do it again?

JOSH
What?

CORINNE
The—the

JOSH
The beard thing?
(She nods, almost hungrily.
He rubs his beard slowly on the microphone, side to side.)

CORINNE
I want one.

JOSH
You can have mine.
Any time you want.
(He approaches the mic and this time rubs his beard on the mic with more—um—vigor. She almost smiles.)

JOSH
Can I hug you?
(She doesn't answer. So, he hugs her. Very slowly and gently. They stay very still in the hug. Then she lets out a tiny squeak.)

CORINNE
*

(Josh's eyes open but he doesn't move from the hug, doesn't want to break the spell.)
Corinne lets out three more squeaks.)

CORINNE
* * *

JOSH *(still not moving)*
Are you okay?

CORINNE *(so so quietly)*
I'm exhausted.
(Then the squeaks come out full flood)

CORINNE
* * * * * * * * * * * * * * *
* * * * * * * * * * * * * * *

(Then Josh, understanding that some kind of release is happening, joins her. They squeak together. It's like crying, but also a little orgasmic.)

JOSH/CORINNE
* * * * * * * * * * * * * *
* * * * * * * * * * * * * *
* * * * * * * * * * * * * *
* * * * * * * * * * * * * *
* * * * * * * * * * * * * *

(Then the release comes to an end. They rest like that.)
CORINNE
Thank you.

End of play.

HEADSTANDING
Jaya Spier

LEFT-HAND AUTO
Anne Boaden

"Commencing... Down, left, idle, turn."

I am apprehensive of the left-hand autorotation, mostly because we don't practice them often. It's silly, really, as helicopter pilots should be as proficient with left-hand autos as right, but the traffic pattern is normally to the right, so there you go.

"Turns, ball, airspeed... A little ball, okay, airspeed..." Looking up through my tinted visor, I find my spot on the runway and set up for the 180-degree auto.

"200 feet, collective full down..." The helo looks good.

"...Coming up on 100 feet..." Ground rush makes the tarmac scream past my periphery. The rubbery smell of old airplane touchdowns invades my nostrils.

"Level, pause..."

"Pull."

I am going to crash.

The moment crystalizes in the stillness before catastrophe, then rewinds and loops through itself ad nauseam, replaying inside my skull like a tic.

The Cobra is supposed to respond the same way. Like swinging a tennis racquet and knowing where the ball will land before it actually touches the clay surface, an aviator anticipates the bird. It's called staying ahead of the aircraft. The engines will spool up, the helicopter will stop falling, and the gauges will return to green. The pilot will surface on the other side of this emergency procedure unscathed.

But I don't.

I try to diagnose the problem, except I'm not sure where to focus. I had been scanning outside the cockpit, picking up on visual clues about airspeed, height above ground, and aircraft yaw. As I glance inside, my eyes search for answers. I fixate on a needle moving fast and in the wrong direction.

Whop-whooop-whooooooop!

I hear this noise over my confusion. The deeper-than-normal slap of the wide aluminum blades punishing the air registers as unusually loud and much too slow. This must be a trick, taken from a Hollywood B-movie about 'Nam.

I am going to crash.

There is no panic inside my skull. There is no time to be afraid. I freeze on the controls out of confusion or perhaps the knowledge that there is nothing I can do. I watch the fat blades bisect the sunlight streaming into my cockpit. My ears quit working or my tinnitus blocks out everything else. I can't tell.

The needle that caught my eye is Nr, rotor RPM. We have a saying: Nr is life. It is the parachute over our heads, the life-force of our spinning death trap. To lose Nr is to acquire the properties of a falling rock. No amount of skill or luck will save you then.

Time crawls forward.

If there had been a cockpit voice recorder, it might have picked up the rapid breathing of my instructor and me.

The Cobra's skids prang off the surface of the cracked cement.

Reality crashes in, hard, as if I'm suddenly woken from a dream. I have been trying to land this auto. My training has kicked in, and I am making all the moves to plant the bird on the runway.

My instructor is not.

He grabs a fistful of throttle from each engine and twists sharply. The skinny helo sparks back to life, jerking her nose drunkenly to the right. I am staring at a wall of pine trees, the side of Runway 4-22. My body rides the bird's altered momentum in disbelief.

Lurching like a wounded animal, the gunship lumbers groggily toward the sky. She feels raw, disconnected. She bucks like a washing machine gone rogue. My first panicked thoughts of fire, smoke, and broken blades slip into my head. Unanticipated Right Yaw emergency procedures flash across my vision.

We gain altitude unwillingly, metal groaning, rotors smacking the air around us. The gauges must be fluctuating, climbing. The cacophony of noise grows as my hearing returns.

"You have the controls, sir."

It's the most basic sentence any pilot learns. Crew coordination in a tandem cockpit is paramount. We cannot see each other. We must talk.

"I have the controls." He bites these words out through gritted teeth. He is willing the helicopter up and over the trees. I realize he has been fighting for the controls for thirty seconds.

We clear the tree line. There is safety in altitude. There

is no runway to crash into up here. We have defied gravity.

"Are... are you okay?" I feel stupid asking this question, but it rolls off my tongue. My endorphins are racing.

"...I think so," he replies. His voice sounds tinny through my helmet.

I know we have just avoided something terrible. I scan the instruments for fluctuations. Every dial is in the green. The Cobra is flying bright and happy, be-bopping along like normal. The chunky rotors split the air with steady chops. We are headed back to base.

"Sir, I think I know what happened."

Silence.

"I... I forgot to roll the throttles up."

Admitting to any mistake is hard, but especially one you have never made before. The maneuver is standard. I've flown hundreds of autos. Bringing the throttles back online is what makes a practice auto a practice.

My instructor makes the call to Tower. We're five minutes out.

"I thought you cracked them," he says.

I don't respond. I am ashamed of my mistake, but also uneasy at the lack of flight hours I received over the past year. But, I shouldn't have forgotten. I was no longer the new kid on the block. I had deployed to a combat zone, twice. I was looking forward to becoming an instructor pilot soon. I was no longer sure that would happen.

We land, taxi, and shut down in stillborn silence.

THE USE OF AN UNRELIABLE NARRATOR IN VLADIMIR NABOKOV'S LOLITA
Pamela Moore Dionne

Lolita opens with a foreword written as though it is a factual statement made by a living person named John Ray, Jr. The statement is made about Humbert Humbert whose story he has published. There is a clear unreliability of narration in this opening foray as witnessed by the name Jon Ray, Jr. with its repeated JR format mirroring the main character Humbert Humbert's repetitive name. Beyond that, readers are aware that Humbert is a fictional character in a fictional storyline though the foreword is written as though what follows is nonfiction. Because of these clear indicators, there is no mistaking that this foreword is part of the fiction. As we begin Humbert's first-person narrative we recognize the ways in which John Ray's speech pattern foreshadows the hyperbole of Humbert's in order to make a point of the fictionality of the forward and the subsequent narrative. Take, for instance, the opening sentence of the foreword, *"Lolita, or the Confessions of a White Widowed Male," such were the two titles under which the writer of the present note received the strange pages it perambulates* (1). There is nothing straightforward in this sentence. John Ray, Jr's approach to a statement about a manuscript he received with two possible titles written as a confession could have been delivered far more succinctly. So we are made aware of the conceit and move forward into a novel that we will read with an ear for the overblown statement as a cautionary guideline.

The question that I ask myself is why would any author want to use a narrative point of view that dances away from truth? Is there a purpose to be served in using this as a device? By the end of the novel, I found some good reasons to employ an untruthful narrator. The way truth is obscured by this type of narration actually characterizes the narrator within the novel's storyline. In the case of Humbert Humbert we are presented with a man who is adept at justifying what he wants and explaining away his own doubts while actually alerting ours. The unreliable narrator creates doubt that can more fully control a reader's response to character and plot. This device works better at involving the reader than an omniscient point-of-view narrative that leaves nothing to speculation. It also works better than a more distanced third person narrative where individual characters have only their own views and prejudices from which to tell a portion of the overall narrative. These observations by peers can be just as flawed as a deliberately unreliable narrative while also being less subtle and possibly far less telling.

As we move into the main body of the novel, we are given more clues about the use of unreliable narration as a tool. For instance, on the opening page of chapter one, we are introduced to the hyperbole in Humbert's speech patterns when he opens with, *Lolita, light of my life, fire of my loins. My sin, my soul. Lo-lee-ta...* (7) This hyperbole is a slant mirror of the foreword's over-the-top language. Each approach seems to have the purpose of distancing the character from his statements. The way the introductory narrative does this is by dancing around J.R.'s topic with overly formal language. Humbert does something similar throughout the novel by preening and ducking in and out of overly constructed language as well as foreign words and portmanteaus that serve to highlight cleverness rather than truth. What this also does is reveal his eccentricity, making him a memorable character.

Nabokov's unreliable narrator may be the best example of this device in modern literature. I reread this particular novel after having read it when I was a teenager. As a young person, I didn't recognize the value of Nabokov's treatment; however, I now see what a narrator who cannot *tell the truth the whole truth and nothing but the truth* may actually add to a novel's layering. While Humbert explains himself as a victim of love, he objectifies Lolita as a nymphet temptress. This is what causes readers to separate from identification with Humbert and judge him harshly. We lose sight of Lolita as anything other than innocent child/victim. What this does once we learn of Lolita's involvement with the meaner-spirited pedophile Clare Quilty is make us question all the assumptions we built over the course of reading *Lolita*.

I read one statement claiming Nabokov attempts to encourage readers to sympathize with Humbert rather than Lolita. My experience is not so much sympathy for Humbert but a recognition that he is a complex of feelings and justifications, which allow him to perpetrate a crime against a young girl whose character is equally as complex as Humbert's. The unreliability of Humbert's narrative is what gave me the chance to step back and judge this character as a bad man while gradually coming to an awareness of factors on Lolita's side of the equation. Her truth is not revealed until late in the plot line because she stands at a remove from the narration. In *Lolita* truth evolves slowly through the limited point of view of a man who cannot be trusted to recognize what he is experiencing. This is what makes the narrative work. It is how we find some sympathy for a man whom we would not otherwise consider worthy.

LAST NIGHT
Jaya Spier

HIS BODY, MY REGRET
Smith Elder

I miss your shirt. It was a faithful soldier
holding the line against my ache.
Now I must surrender,
and we must have our days, and I must dream
combing through basement memories, scraps of you—
your muttered melodies and your casual grin,
your affection cascading carelessly behind you—
things you do not even know I own.

The smoke thickens. Your thick hair dries,
your hand passing over it a message: *Yourtimeisup*.
And yet I cannot forget you, my lonely ghost,
your fragile eyes beholding your wild center
and drawing back, terrified
by the violence of your need—for what,
even you do not know.

REDEMPTION
Stacie Jenkins Townsend

you see my soul
this is our truth since the first time you
held my gaze
and I cast my spell on you
a witchery born of
heartache and passion

embarrassed by your attention
I said there was no chemistry
embarrassed by my attraction
I said we were not lovers
but chemistry and love was
all we were

desire buzzed through me at the
sound of your voice
smell of your neck
utter of my name
uncertainty pulled me into your
soft chest and I disappeared
our souls had kindred recognition
you saw me like no one had
I got so lost I knew
when you left me I'd never be found
apart we were incomplete
together almost whole but broken

we fit together like two
well used puzzle pieces
my backside rounded into the
cavern of your paunch
my wild haired head nestled under your chin

our bodies sighed into a perfect fit

your arm twice my length slid under me
my head rested in its crook
my hand in yours as if it found home
huge strong fingers slipped over mine
dark covered light
still there was calmness and peace

your other arm held me tight to you
under my breast
under my heart
under my soul
even with the crushing weight of you
I still inhaled I still exhaled

legs entwined over under over under
my short legs didn't need to stretch
to anchor my feet atop your
fuzzy giant size 15's
I leaned into you like you were my cross
you gripped me like I was your savior

ADAPTATION: NEW EYES
Kimi Hardesty

I returned there, after eighteen months without you, and what seemed like
only a flash of time in the Southwest.
It was no different than before, the creek, with the ducks and the water splitting
in that one place and the branches reaching and the limestone slick with algae.
I returned there, to see if there was change at the creek that might mirror me.

Me with new eyes, a new body, in which to take in the view.

The split of the water into two smaller streams remained, and the ducks still quacked
and waddled and dipped their heads below the creek's surface.
The limestone, still slick and green and the branches extended over the water.
The cardinals still there.

I saw no difference there other than the new growth and the brush and the trees
taller, an adaptation of the eyes.

WRITING AS A MEANS OF ACCEPTING A DISABILITY
Diana Smith Rush

There are many memoirs that focus on disability. Some are told by the person with the disability, such as *Planet of the Blind* by Stephen Kuusisto, while others are told from the point of view of someone experiencing it secondhand, like Emily Rapp writes in *The Still Point of the Turning World*. Whether written by a parent with a disabled child, a spouse with a disabled partner or an adult child of a disabled parent, it can be easy to fall into the trap of writing about the experience as a burden. The inclination is to focus on the difficulties and become resentful towards the person you are caring for or the disability itself.

These memoirs have avoided that tendency. Through honest telling of their personal journeys, they express the difficulty of their situations without looking for pity from their readers. Their intentions in writing their stories are clear. They both write to figure out how to cope with disease and disability and its effect on their lives, as they journey from denial to attempts at acceptance.

Though these memoirs are similarly themed, their challenges are very different. In *Planet of the Blind,* Kuusisto writes firsthand of life as a man who is almost completely blind. He comes full circle from concealing his near blindness and pretending it isn't real, to accepting that with help he can lead a richer life. "Delicate, skinny, inordinately active, I was sharpening a sixth sense that fostered the impression in my parents and almost everyone else that I could see far better than I really could." (11)

Kuusisto details life starting with his childhood and how

it felt to have his parents want to hide his disability. It would be many years before he acknowledges his blindness and allows people to help him. Throughout the book, he never seeks the sympathy of the reader. His only need is to share his own pursuit towards acceptance:

> And so, I shave and take an aspirin. Then I call the telephone operator and ask for the number for the New York State Commission for the Blind. I need help walking.
>
> I've needed help all my life.
>
> It's that simple. (Kuusisto 143)

His intention is to document the journey he took moving through difficult circumstances. He wrote to process, to explain and to try to find acceptance, but never to complain or ask for solicitude. Instead of a burden, the author sees his disability as an opportunity to triumph. "I would conquer space by hurtling through it. I wore telescopic glasses, suffered from crushing headaches, but still chose to ride a bicycle - with nothing more than adrenaline for assurance" (Kuusisto 8).

Despite his disability, the author studies writing in college and graduate school and later teaches writing. He recognizes it as a kind of salvation from his disability:

> The classroom, however, is my ray of light. The Bible says there is a fatness in heaven, a rich sweetness where the soul can feast. Sharing stories with my students becomes a kind of mutual tasting I encourage them to read to me, and they do. Not just their own stories but the things they find at random in the library. Talking in this way, we find we can make something larger, you might call it growing room.

(Kuusisto 133)

His appreciation for the written word, and its impact on his life, is made more evident by the placement of quotes from works of poetry or prose, to open each section of the book. He used these references to other writing to assist in putting words to his feelings.

In comparison, Emily Rapp, writes *The Still Point of the Turning World,* from the perspective of mothering a disabled child. Specifically, she writes as a mother who was just told of her baby's terminal disease. She never completely comes to terms with her son's diagnosis but is able to appreciate the time she has with him and enjoy what he is able to do. "After those first few weeks of blackness and bouncing back and forth in the void, I realized that I didn't want to be coddled or protected from the wild unpredictability of my feelings. I wanted to work, laugh, write, be, *live*" (Rapp 125). Rapp isn't able to reach a complete acceptance of her son's diagnosis because her ending would eventually be the death of her son and not the beginning of a new, more positive future.

Like Kuusisto, her reason to tell her story is based on the need to write to get through this impossible time. "Writers scribbling in the midst of grief have noted the ways in which writing about the experience from the inside creates something new, namely, a safe or safe-ish place to rest. A net, a landing point, a dock from which to view the turbulent and troubled water without having to wade in it every moment of every day. In a word: relief" (Rapp 124).

Emily Rapp finished her book with a message of a triumph as well. In her case it was more about acquiescence than true acceptance, yet she was able to find a way to cope with her impending loss. "Because I know, in whatever final lucid moment I have before I die, I will see Ronan's face, and I will wish I could hold him one last time before I, too, am released from this body and make my own crossing from this life into whatever comes next" (Rapp 249). She knew she had to deal with the end of her baby's short life and had prepared herself for that time. Her realization of those forthcoming feelings, help her imagine what it will be like when her own time comes to die. Her hope is that she will be writing until the end and that the writing itself will have eased her there gently. "And I would continue scribbling, hoping it would help me reach the end intact or sane, and I did it knowing that any scribble might be my last" (249).

As she worked through the emotions of her son's unavoidable death, Rapp turned to reading for comfort. In her memoir, like Kuusisto, she used lines from poetry and prose throughout her work. "And as if the ghost of Emily Dickinson were speaking directly into my ear, I remembered these lines: *I felt a Cleaving in my Mind / As if my Brain had split. / I tried to match it --Seam by Seam-- / But could not make it fit*" (Rapp 5). She placed them in her piece to illuminate the impact of reading in her life as a means to define her feelings.

Rapp frequently discusses her own writing and reading as a necessary outlet as she faces her own reality. *In Still Point of the* Turning World, Rapp had people in her life that encouraged her to write when she first heard her son's diagnosis. She felt like she should be grieving and not writing, yet writing called to her as an outlet from what she was experiencing: "In those first hellish weeks, I had to write; that was all there was. That was living. (My friend Lisa, also a writer and one schooled in the ways of grief, called me every day. *Write!* she urged. *Do it right now!)* (Rapp 124).

Although they wrote from two different perspectives on disability, there were many similarities to how Rapp's and Kuusisto's stories were told and experienced. Despite the weight of disability and disease on their lives, Kuusisto and Rapp discovered ways to prevail. They were at first unable to deal with their challenges, but learned through writing that they could not only begin to process, but overcome the difficult roads before them.

They shared multiple techniques in telling their stories but, in the end, their outcomes are very different. Kuusisto learns to work with his disability and, in doing so, begins to lead a fuller, richer life. Rapp learns to write through her hurt and embrace her remaining time with her son. Neither was searching for sympathy from the reader. They were both simply writing to navigate their way through impossible circumstances and share their victories with readers.

Kuusisto, Stephen. *Planet of the Blind*. New York: Dial, 1998.

Rapp, Emily. *The Still Point of the Turning World*. New York: The Penguin Press, 2013.

DAY'S END
Tisha Gentry

Evening lingers inviting the invisible
to dance in fading light

Moved by the quiet, I grow still

Breathing in the memory of cut grass and long ago greens
I am 17 again on the plains of my youth

I can smell my mother mowing
I can see him swinging

They are no longer them though
Their days have grown short

The moment is full of time
Now, and then

Bending, I tee my ball
An unseen curtsy to all that was and is

The sound cracks the silence
I have found the fairway

FOCUS ON
Stacie Jenkins Townsend

GROWING
Kimi Hardesty

I.

It should take more than a change in identity
to alter the inner core, destroy it.
To be held that loosely, a disgrace.
The foundation built of rock is stronger
than the one made of dreams.
What would the goddess, Anat, think?
She, who seized Mot and cut him with a sickle,
and winnowed him, she who scorched him and crushed him
with a mill, leaving his flesh for the birds?

She would feel disappointment.

Mot got what he deserved.
Some would call it karma.

II.

Lightning strikes the highest peaks.
Exposure kills there, not in the valleys of soft green,
where the limes grow and the bird sings.
The mind imposes death and then withdraws it as the village
hues the skin, gives sustenance within its boundaries. I hold it.

III.

It is true you can be raised from the dead.
A change in identity need only be a sloughing of the skin
and with it, new armor, the core neither cracked nor defeated.
All eyes watching as you show the village your strength.

And that village holds me, carries me like a current, only
the water is not cold.

SHAME
Tisha Gentry

TO HIS OTHERS
Smith Elder

I understand the touch of your desire.
Of course I do.
|I have felt it in my fingertips, my hips
I have felt it flooding slowly through my skin,
no sense of sin
only soft delicious light.
I have felt his heat beside me in the night
and slept against his heartbeat.
I know the fire.

So, your bright-shadow fingerprints upon his skin
do me no injury.
The ways you shape his history
have made him who he is,
have given him a good and gentle beauty
a strength, a confidence,
a tenderness that washes through me--
breaks down my defenses,
enters into me.
Where your delights have ended, mine begin.

But though I keep him in my heart, he is not mine.
His hands have left their mark;
the bruises bright and clean, the hidden symbols--
though fingers, teeth and leather never scarred--
and still I taste those moments in the dark
his rhythm hard,
insistent, pressing, deep and slick,
my body tense and epileptic.

Yet, I am not part of his design.

He shapes me but he did not make me. I remain
my own, myself, some part of me still free
submitting, willing, but unowned
my every nerve alive, and following his lead, but me
a passenger, only enthroned
in ecstasy a moment.
That moment is not mine, though I alone
have felt it in my veins.
This vivid bliss should never serve as chains.
His pleasure is not mine to keep, nor give --
Possessing him could only cause him pain.

I can begrudge him nothing. And I trust
(for choosing me, I know he chooses well)
that you, his others, hold him as I do
in honest view
and shine beneath the motion of his hands
and scream and weep and shake when he commands
and smile to see him sleep.
Your beauty cannot conquer mine
or alter what he sees behind my eyes,
but only make the gentle rise

of breath inside him all the sweeter sight
for sharing it with others who have seen it in the light
and smiled at the whisper of his voice,
his tongue tasting your name,
your body answering his touch with lust.

So, touch him if you will. My fingers trail behind.
Let us smudge each other's fingerprints with kisses
and laugh, ignoring smaller people's hisses.
Let them mock, and miss our pleasure. I don't mind.

I-5 HEAVEN
Stacie Jenkins Townsend

HYBRID AS AN EXPRESSION OF EMPATHY
Alana Jamison

As with most words in the English language, the word "truth" carries more than one meaning. It can mean a fact that is accepted as true. It can express a firm belief like a religious belief in a supernatural entity. It can imply emotional experience, a relative truth in the sense that what is being expressed as "true" supports a kind of general abstract of all things human. In literature, truth falls under the categories "non-fiction" and "fiction," but in other genres like poetry and hybrid, this truth is not so easy to label.

Jacqueline Kolosov writes about this in her article "Finding the Right Form: Exploring and Experimenting with Hybrid Literary Genres":

> Because they resist the impulse to classify, hybrid literary genres both challenge and enlarge ways of thinking about genre, and can prompt analysis and interrogation of such aspects of literary art as syntax, setting, and character, as well as more philosophical questions centered on the nature of truth, identity, and memory. (Kolosov 63)

By comparing and contrasting the hybrid work of Kazim Ali in *Bright Felon,* Marguerite Duras in *The Lover,* and Bhanu Kapil in *Ban en Banlieue,* we will develop a discussion about truth and storytelling in hybrid. Specifically, how the freedom of truth's expression within the form affects the writer's and reader's perceptions of the work.

For the sake of the discussion, we will speculate a bit about the kinds of truth expressed in these works and acknowledge that while the "I" does not always (or even usually) imply an authorial perspective, here it often does: In *Bright Felon*, Kazim Ali uses hybrid to incorporate memoir into poetry to engage the reader in the difficulties of the changing self. Christopher Henessy writes the following about Ali and Ali's book *Bright Felon*:

> Here is a poet of non-narrative experimentation suddenly faced with speaking autobiographical truths; a young gay Muslim negotiating his personal, familial and religious view of homosexuality. *Bright Felon*'s interest in silence shows the book to be as much a coming out memoir as it is poetic discourse on the act of coming out. (28)

In *The Lover*, Marguerite Duras incorporates memoir into fiction to tell the story of a young life growing towards a fuller self through trauma. In French, Duras' work is *l'autofiction*, a "combination of autobiographical writing with an insistence on the freedoms of fiction" (Lee). As a work of French literature, *The Lover* accomplishes something that English literature can only label as hybrid. Jeffery S. Staley and Laurie Edson write in their literary criticism "Objectifying the Subjective: The Autobiographical Act of Duras's *The Lover*":

> How Duras chooses to regard the girl growing up in Vietnam, what emotions she believes herself to have felt, cannot rely on objective reality, but only upon subjective representation of that self, the young girl. Any question of the text's "truth" (which might try to assert the narrative as fiction) fails to recognize that the text means to write about how Duras views herself, how Duras desires to relate her identity in the past as well as in the present. (288)

In *Ban enBanliue*Bhanu Kapil uses hybrid to blur the lines of memoir, poetry, and fiction to create a challenging piece that addresses both the form of writing and the content it creates, specifically the trauma of being outcast. The following statements are made in a review of *Ban en Banlieue* in Publishers Weekly:

> Though Ban is fictional, her historical context is not; the immigrant suburbs of late-1970s London function both as a setting and manner of "detailing—which is to say: scouring/burnishing—the world [Kapil] grew up in." . . . the porous relationship between Ban's story and the story of Kapil writing and thinking about Ban is fundamental throughout. (58, 59)

Each of these three pieces address the truth and self. They are intensely personal accounts; however, the hybrid genre allows the author some distance from his or her subject while it simultaneously gives the reader an intimate view of the author's life and thoughts. When authors like Ali, Duras, and Kapil use hybrid to push deeper into his or her own experiences whether factual or not, the reader is carried along into the sacred, into a belief. Sometimes that belief is damaging, which may be why the author confronts it, but the hybrid form allows the writer to flex through this. In these hybrid works, a reader can find fiction, memoir, and poetry mingling together to create multiple ways for an author to challenge and engage both themselves and the reader.

Discovering the Self

In *Bright Felon*, Kazim Ali presents his readers with a kind of autobiography within the lines of hybrid poetry. As hybrid, Ali blurs the lines of poetry, prose, and memoir. At times, his story reads like prose, moving the reader along through lines of narrative. At other times, Ali reveals his emotion through broken sentences and lines of poetry.

> There is no place in the Quran which requires acts of homosexuality to be punishable by lashings and death.
>
> *Hadith* or scripture. Scripture or rupture.
>
> Should I travel out from under the blanket. (Ali 88)

It is a serious game of show and tell where Ali deals with his broken identity as both a Muslim and a homosexual man, exposing his darkest secrets to tell about the most difficult moments of his life.

Set in the French colony of Saigon, Marguerite Duras tells the story of a young girl that centers around an image of Duras at fifteen years old on a ferry. *The Lover* is a novel that reads like a memoir. The nameless "I" becomes clearer and more personal as the story moves along, and the central themes of family, trauma, and loss expound as a transformation in the life of this young woman. Maxine Hong Kingston writes as an introduction, "*The Lover* is a story about girl and woman becoming artist. I feel all right about taking this fiction as Marguerite Duras's autobiography" (Kingston vii). Maybe it is difficult to read this book as fiction because the imagery the author uses draws us into her emotions at a specific place and time.

Bhanu Kapil writes a novel that is not a novel, a novel of poetry set within late-1970s England that centers on the author's creation of a character who manifests as a people.

> What is born in England but is never English?" What grew a tail? What leaned over and rested its hands on its knees? An immigrant has a set of complex origins, is

from elsewhere; the monster is made, on the other hand, from local mixtures of organic and inorganic materials, repurposed teeth, selenium, lungs, pink lightning, public health concerns. (Kapil 21)

Ban en banlieueis a fictional character that embodies truth regarding race and gender. "The more time passed, the less and less was Ban. Something that could be written down" (Kapil 24). Kapil catches the reader up in the drama of Ban a truthful hybrid account of life in the outskirts.

Ali, Duras, and Kapil express a vulnerability in their work that draws the reader deeper into its truth. Ali expresses this in an interview with Christopher Hennessy:

> We are, each of us, flawed creatures, aren't we? We stumble, we fail, we make terrible mistakes again. Beautiful flawed humans we are and in that divine. I can't think of any virtue more noble than compassion. *Bright Felon* was a confession of desperate measure but was written from the heart as an emotional outpouring.

Perhaps the confrontation of a belief in these hybrid works presents an opportunity for the author and the reader to heal. Is this the extension of compassion that Ali speaks of? Duras, Ali, and Kapil all seem to be addressing difficult and personal ideas.

In a way, these authors are reaching out to their readers asking that they embrace the authors' knowledge of life, asking that they engage with that knowledge in an effort to heal humanity. Again, Ali expresses this in an interview with Christopher Hennessy:

> And we have to figure out a way of being human, of relating to each other and staying alive. We have to

figure out what society means, what civilization means, and what our relationship is to the natural and even the animal world! These things are of critical importance and will determine our future, and I think language, poetry and literature are part of that. (Hennessy 29)

When an author successfully expresses the truth of humanity within themselves, the reader does not feel manipulated, but empathized with. The writer's ability to empathize with the human experience, in turn, allows the reader to empathize with that experience. Hybrid gives the author flexibility to express this in such a way that connects the reader to the truth found their work and even allows the reader to explore their own story within it.

Silence and the Body

Through Hybrid, Kapil moves beyond simply stating facts or emotions to express truth. She expresses truth within both the sound and movement of her poetry and within the literal movements of her body by performing physical acts which accompany her work. For example, lying in the grass as Ban at Pratt Institute in New York. For all three of these authors, trauma to the physical self comes into a play in a profound way that challenges the reader's perceptions and the writer's experience. As an emotional experience, trauma steers the reader's perceptions to connect them to the story.

In a conversation with author Reiko Rizzuto, she said about trauma in fiction, "It's a visceral experience for the reader. We're trying to create a sense of disruption. We're trying to create a testimony." Through each of these works, in their form as hybrid that allows blending fiction with fact, the authors are trying to give the reader "access to their traumatic experience by recreating it" (Rizzuto). In this way the reader can enter the traumatic experience themselves. They must experience it for themselves. The disruption felt by the reader is meant to stir up questions not only about the trauma the author is expressing, but about the trauma in light of the human experience. Humans all experience trauma, but we do not experience the same kind of trauma. Literature exposes us to other's trauma, which offers us empathy.

Trauma in "[t]he memoir is about the personal, and the trauma narrative has a much more historical or cultural reach" (Rizzuto). As hybrid that allows both fiction and fact, the works of Ali and Kapil accomplish this cultural reach through their expression of trauma through factually true events. Again, as hybrid, Ali's work reads as both memoir and poetry. He is introducing the reader to his religious upbringing and the trauma created through his experience with lack of acceptance as a homosexual male in his religious community. Ali's trauma is expressed through his relating the "coming out" experience to the reader through the cultural viewpoint of himself as a Muslim. Though Kapil does include fictional aspects to her work, primarily the character of Ban, the cultural events she writes about are entirely true:

> I would like to present: a list of the errors I made as a poet engaging a novel-shaped space, the space of a book: set: on a particular day and at a particular time: April 23rd, 1979. Thenovel begins at 4 p.m.—just as Ban—a brown [black] girl—is walking home from school. (Kapil 20)

Kapil's work challenges not only our response to trauma, but also the way it is perceived in literature. In the words of Kapil "literature that is not made of literature." Her work uses the fictional character of Ban to deal with the trauma of the race riot, but because she presents it in hybrid, the essence of fact remains, which changes the reader's experience reading the work. Duras also does this:

> She uses the setting around her to symbolize or draw metaphor to her person. She can't say this is how I feel or [express] the situation that she's in, so she uses her setting to do this. In order to get back to herself, she must peel away the layers of falseness. The falseness of those around her: her mother and her brothers. (Rizzuto)

However, in contrast to both Ali and Kapil's work, the events of Duras' work flip the idea expressed by Rizzuto on its head in that what she writes about is generally accepted as a factually true account of her life; however, because it is presented in fiction, the reader cannot assume this, and so is affected by the trauma differently. In a way, as fiction, Duras' work is as Rizzuto says, "when [the writer is] dealing with trauma, [she] wants to pretend it didn't happen. There's pretense." Through fiction, Duras is able to pretend with the reader. Through hybrid, she is able to stand back and look at a particular snapshot of her life. She leads the reader there to experience life with her in colonial Vietnam, life as a white woman in abrown, Asian culture, life pushing against the ideological norms of her youth, to embrace the love of the unexpected.

A coming out of another sort happens for Ali and his reader through his use of setting. In his interview with Christopher Hennessy, Ali talks about the ordinariness of life and how his expression of it in *Bright Felon* changed his writing:

> [N]one of that could have happened without the weird poetic exposure of *Bright Felon*—that *ordinariness* of

> my life in Oberlin, waking before dawn to eat, fasting all day and so on. [So now] I *do* find myself in a really interesting poetic space where I'm actually *in* the world, living—and writing a little more openly, I guess. (Hennessy 30)

For Ali, like Duras, his use of setting helps him to "peel away the falseness." Ali uses his setting throughout his work to steer his reader along the path his life has taken by situating each section of his piece within a specific place and time, and he also uses silence. Each of the authors use silence, whether in choosing to leave certain things unsaid like Duras, or in choosing to relate the silence of culture in a certain situation to create impact like Kapil. Ali talks about silence in his interview with Hennessy:

> The body keeps its silence to protect itself, but silencing the external is also a way of attaining a deeper connection with other beings and with the natural world, the planet itself, which as James Lovelock has taught us, may actually *be* a unified organism. (Hennessy 30)

For each of the authors, the use of silence accomplishes this connection with the reader. In the expression of trauma in Duras' work, this silence enhances the story, providing a break in time, a "traumatic gap" in the narrative. In an interesting way, Duras does this also by speaking into the silence that is the lost image of her youth, the image of her on the ferry. Staley and Edson write about this image, saying, "That is why the image of herself on the ferry is so memorable; it symbolizes a breaking away from her mother's authority and the dawning of Duras's subjectivity" (Staley 292). The silence of bodily stillness creates dramatic impact for the reader in

Kapil's work, as well. She refers to Ban as a monster, lying still on the pavement. She relates Ban to a young woman sexually battered in India, using this person to possess the person of Ban.

The body appears in each of these works to express trauma and truth. Often the honesty within sexual vulnerability that the authors write into their pieces allows the reader to connect even more with the truth the authors wish to express. This is especially true for Kapil, who uses her own body to symbolize the traumatic experiences of Ban. For Duras, the body is used throughout to express sexual autonomy on the part of the main character, and this autonomy is what allows her the freedom to break away from her family.

> For Duras, sexual desire is linked with autonomy, because the child maintains self-possession and literally conducts [hers and the lover's] sexual relations, she refuses to submit to the undertow of masculine desire that seeks to make an object of woman. // Her mother's not wanting her to write is essentially an attempt to deprive her daughter of access to her own sexuality, and thus her autonomy. (Staley 294)

In Ali's work, the body appears to allow the author to ask questions relating to immortality. He asks these questions of himself and of the reader:

> But is it really like Fanny writes, the body only a car the soul is driving. // Or something of us sunk into the matter of the body, part of us actually flesh, inseparable from it and upon death, truly dispersed, smoke. // The body of the prophet's wife always between us. Who said what. // In which case there really is something to

grieve at death: that the soul is wind, not immortal. (Ali 1)

These questions of bodily experience within the works of Ali, Duras, and Kapil impact both the writer and the reader. The use of trauma in hybrid creates an empathetic response, and it creates the perception of a reach across cultures to reveal truth about the human experience.

A Vehicle of Fluidity

Kolosov concludes her essay by reflecting on a particular strength within the hybrid form, which we can use to reflect on the works of Ali, Duras, and Kapil:

> Intrinsically, then, issues of gender, race, class, religion, and political or national identity complicate and enrich the experience of reading the hybrid forms by virtue of the fact that form [. . .] should be an expression of content. Literary hybrids—thematically and structurally—reveal the paradox that identities and genres are constructed and arbitrary, yet simultaneously "real." (Kolosov 74)

The works of Ali, Duras, and Kapil present the reader with a paradox—like with poetry the experiences presented are not necessarily non-fiction or fiction. These experiences the author's present are entirely human. Through shaping the reader's perceptions through the author's perspective—their trauma and physical selves—they allow the reader to live their moments. We walk as though hand in hand with the authors through their experiences and watch the shapes of ourselves be realized. Together, we become real people who need to connect in order to heal.

Work Cited

Primary Sources:

Ali, Kazim. *Bright Felon: Autobiography and Cities*. Reprint edition. Wesleyan, 2012.

Duras, Marguerite. *The Lover*. Pantheon, 1998.

Kapil, Bhanu. *Ban en Banlieue*. Nightboat, 2015.

Secondary Sources:

Ban en Banlieue, by Bhanu Kapil. Publishers Weekly 19 Jan. 2015: 58-59.

Hennessy, Christopher. "An Interview with Kazim Ali." American Poetry Review Vol. 42. Issue 5 (2013): 28-32.

Kolosov, Jacqueline. "Finding the Right Form." *The Writer's Chronicle* Feb. 2016: 63-74.

Lee, Richard. "Fiction v non-fiction—English literature's made-up divide." *The Guardian*. The Guardian, 24 March 2016. Web. 21 April 2016.

Rizzuto, Reiko. "Trauma in Fiction." Goddard College. Goddard College, Clockhouse,

Plainfield, VT. 6 January 2016.

Staley, Jeffrey S. and Edson, Laurie. "Objectifying the Subjective: The Autobiographical Act of Duras's The Lover." Critique Vol. 42 Issue 3 (2001): 287.

MALDIVIAN FISHERMAN
Anne Boaden

CONTRIBUTOR BIOS

Ian August is an award-winning, internationally produced playwright. Full-length plays include: *The Goldilocks Zone*, (Passage Theatre Company), *Donna Orbits the Moon* (NJ Repertory Company, Utah Contemporary Theatre), *Missing Celia Rose* (NYC Summer Play Festival; Orlando Shakespeare Theater's "Playfest 2009"), *Submitted by C. Randall McCloskey* (2011 NY Intl. Fringe Festival), *Natural History* (2009 NY Intl. Fringe Festival), *The Aisling* (2009 Heiress Productions New Play Series Award), *The Moor's Son, Interviewese, The Excavation of Mary Anning, Displaced,* and *Cobble*r. Mr. August's works have been published by Sam French Inc., *The Pitkin Review*, Smith and Kraus Publishing and the One-Act Play Depot.

Anne Boaden is a former attack helicopter pilot in the United States Marine Corps currently working on a memoir of her time on active duty. She lives in England with her husband, six chickens, two cats, and one dog.

Abigail Crittenden is a MFAW G1, and she deeply adores writing about werewolves and retelling myths for a modern audience. She dreams of green hills, clear waters, and prays to never see Artemis bathing, for she does not wish to share Actaeon's fate.

Jessica Dickey is an award-winning actor and playwright most known for her play THE AMISH PROJECT. Other produced/published works include CHARLES IVES TAKE ME HOME and ROW AFTER ROW. Her new play THE REMBRANDT is currently being produced at Steppenwolf Theater Company. Jessica is currently commissioned by Manhattan Theatre Club, Ford's Theatre, and ShadowCatcher. As an actor she was most recently seen at Playwrights

Horizons, the Humana Festival, and the tv show HOMELAND. She is a resident of New Dramatists.

Poet and writer **Pamela Moore Dionne's** work has appeared in a number of journals including *Shenandoah* and *Pontoon*. She was a Jack Straw writer and received their Artist Support Grant to record a CD of her Sabina Spielrein Ghazal series. Dionne earned a Centrum residency and an Artist Trust Gap Grant. Her visual art has been published in journals and presented in one-woman shows. Other credits include founding and managing the online art & literature journal *Literary Salt*. She was also the founder of Discovery Bay Games.

Smith Elder works in several genres, including fiction, poetry, and drama. She graduated from Illinois Wesleyan University in 2012 with a BA in Theatre Arts and is currently in her first semester at Goddard College. Her work often focuses on stories of morality and marginalization in speculative fiction settings. She lives in Chicago with her partner, two cats, and a ferret.

Terry Finley is a writer, a ponderer of the unpondered, a vehicle for the muse who doesn't truly exist except as the light the stars chase to their demise.

Tisha Gentry lives in Orlando, Florida. She loves writing and golf, but not alligators.

Kimi Hardesty is a writer, photographer and world traveler who lives in Lexington, KY. She is currently earning her MFA at Goddard College, where she was the recipient of the Engaged Artist Award. Kimi has been a past Assistant Editor for the print journal *Profane*.

Alana Jamison is in her final semester in Goddard College's low residency MFA in creative writing program where she has worked with writers Beatrix Gates, Jan Clausen, Bhanu Kapil, and Rebecca Brown. She writes the blog "It's Simple" for Tulsa Kids Magazine and her story "What I Lost" is forthcoming in Flash: The International Short Story Magazine. She Lives in Tulsa, Oklahoma with her husband and two children.

Aaron W. Kiser is a poet who loves and appreciates the universe while trying to be a constant observer of all things. He enjoys cruising through life with his wife, kids, cats, and dog.

Scott Morris is an Outdoor Educator across the American West. He enjoys reading on the banks of alpine lakes.

Diana Smith Rush is the mother of six and grandmother to one. After receiving her undergraduate degree from the University of Nebraska at Omaha, she took a twenty-one-year hiatus from writing before she decided to return to school for her Master's. She is currently writing a memoir about raising a child with an intellectual disability.

Jennifer Skura is an American-born artist who has worked in a variety disciplines, including theatre, film, and visual arts for over 30 years. She received her B.F.A. from Sam Houston State University in theatre and is an M.F.A. creative writing candidate at Goddard College. Her work has been presented in Los Angeles, New York City, and throughout the northeast. Member SAG-AFTRA/AEA/DG/HRC.

Jaya Spier is a writer living in the Pacific Northwest. She spends her time reading, traveling, and walking her poodle.

Brett Townsend lives in Port Townsend, Washington with his wife, two sons, two dogs, one cat, and six chickens. He is currently working on a collection of short stories loosely based on the events of his life.

Stacie Jenkins Townsend has been published in *The Salmon Creek Journal* at Washington State University-Vancouver, *The Pitkin Review*, *The Columbian Newspaper*, Somnambulist zine, and has two neglected blogs. These achievements are lovely, but pale in comparison to her three teenagers, significant person, two cats, many friends, and family members who tremble in fear every time Stacie says, "I'm writing a memoir!" She is currently working on an uplifting collection of essays about her life dealing with addiction, depression, love, and heartbreak. She'd like to dedicate this publication to her Write or Die Otter Gang who keep her going.

Victoria Veldhoen tests for rare diseases in itty bitty babies during the day and writes about oddities (real or imagined) during the night.

Made in the USA
Columbia, SC
03 December 2017